Fabu... FIBONACCI NUMBERS

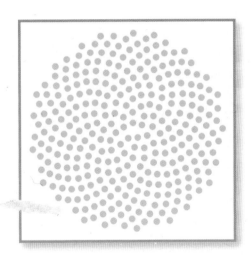

by Mary Lindeen

HOUGHTON MIFFLIN   BOSTON

Printed in China

ISBN 10: 0-618-89984-7
ISBN 13: 978-0-618-89984-5

23456789 NOR 16 15 14 13 12 11 10 09 08

Leonardo Fibonacci

Leonardo da Vinci is not the only famous Leonardo from Italy. Another Leonardo was born in Pisa, Italy. He would become one of the most famous mathematicians in history.

Leonardo Fibonacci was born more than 800 years ago, in 1175. This is the same year workers in Pisa began building a tower. Today, that tower is a famous landmark. Have you ever heard of the Leaning Tower of Pisa? If you visit the tower today, you will find a statue of Leonardo Fibonacci right across the street.

Leonardo Fibonacci's father was a merchant. His work took him to different places. When Leonardo's father was assigned to a job in Algiers, Africa, his son went with him. Leonardo received most of his education in Algiers. It was also where he learned about Hindu Arabic numbers.

At that time, European people used Roman numerals. Fibonacci introduced Europe to the Hindu Arabic numbering system, which is the system we use today. He discovered that this system was easier for merchants to use when buying and selling. He also discovered that the system was much easier to use for solving math problems.

Roman Numerals and Arabic Numbers			
I	1	XL	40
II	2	L	50
III	3	XC	90
IV	4	C	100
V	5	D	500
X	10	M	1,000

Read·Think·Write How would you write these numbers using Roman numerals? 10, 15, 55

The Fibonacci Series

One of Fibonacci's most famous mathematical discoveries is called the Fibonacci series. This is a special pattern of numbers. It is formed by adding two numbers in the series to get the next number.

The series begins with 0 and 1. Then you keep adding the last two numbers in the series to get the next number. So:

$$0 + 1 = 1$$
$$1 + 1 = 2$$
$$1 + 2 = 3$$
$$2 + 3 = 5$$

The first six numbers in the Fibonacci series are:

0, 1, 1, 2, 3, 5

Let's keep going to see what comes next.

$$3 + 5 = 8$$
$$5 + 8 = 13$$
$$8 + 13 = 21$$
$$13 + 21 = 34$$

Read·Think·Write Can you figure out what the next three numbers in the series will be?

0, 1, 1, 2, 3, 5, 8, 13, 21, 34, _____, _____, _____

When you cut an apple through the middle, you can see the five seed cavities.

6

Fibonacci in Nature

Through the years, people have found Fibonacci numbers in many items in the natural world.

Inside many fruits and vegetables, you will find an example of a Fibonacci number in nature.

Look at the apple. When it is cut in half, how many seed cavities, or spaces for seeds, do you see?

You might count the seed cavities in other fruits and vegetables. In each case, the number of seed cavities matches one of the numbers in the Fibonacci series.

If you count the petals on some flowers, you will find Fibonacci numbers. Here are some examples:

Iris	3 petals
Primrose	5 petals
Ragwort	13 petals
Daisy	34, 55, or 89 petals

(Keep in mind that animals sometimes eat flower petals, or sometimes a petal gets torn off or falls off. If you decide to try this, make sure you have a "perfect" flower, or count several flowers and figure out the average number of petals.)

It's not only flower petals that match Fibonacci numbers. Look closely at the seeds on this sunflower. Notice that the seeds make two spiral patterns. One set of short spirals moves out clockwise from the center of the flower. Another set of longer spirals goes counterclockwise.

The seeds in a sunflower grow in a pattern like the ones shown here.

8

If you were to count the number of short spirals and the number of long spirals, you would get two different totals. But both would be Fibonacci numbers. You might have 21 clockwise spirals and 34 counterclockwise spirals, or 34 clockwise spirals and 55 counterclockwise spirals. No matter what the total, it will be a Fibonacci number.

A pinecone also has two sets of spirals. It has overlapping "leaves" that are called bracts. The bracts form spiral patterns. One set of spirals goes from the bottom to the top of the pinecone. Another set goes around the pinecone.

If you count the up-and-down spirals, you will end up with a Fibonacci number. If you count the spirals going around, you will end up with a Fibonacci number. And no matter what those two numbers are, they will always be numbers that are next to each other in the Fibonacci series.

Read·Think·Write What are two examples in nature that have a double spiral pattern that matches the Fibonacci numbers?

Fibonacci numbers, spirals, and nature are connected in other ways. Look at the rectangle on the right. It is made up of a spiral of small boxes that gradually get larger to

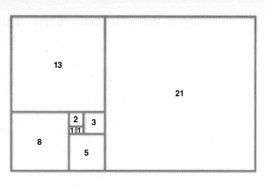

form one large rectangle. First, notice the spiral pattern of the boxes as they start small and get larger.

Now look at the numbers that have been added in each box.

Let's do the math.

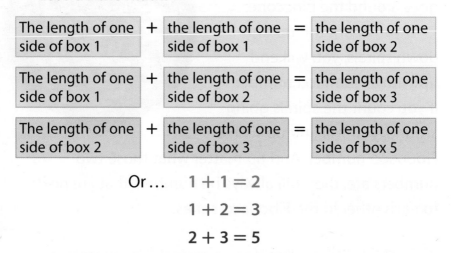

The length of one side of box 1	+	the length of one side of box 1	=	the length of one side of box 2
The length of one side of box 1	+	the length of one side of box 2	=	the length of one side of box 3
The length of one side of box 2	+	the length of one side of box 3	=	the length of one side of box 5

Or ...

$$1 + 1 = 2$$
$$1 + 2 = 3$$
$$2 + 3 = 5$$

Does that look familiar? It's the Fibonacci series. What is the pattern of the numbers in the boxes?

Look at this snail shell. This kind of shell is called a nautilus shell. If you cut it in half, you can see a spiral pattern.

Now look what happens when you put the Fibonacci rectangle on top of the shell's spiral pattern. Notice how the spaces in the shell match the boxes in the Fibonacci rectangle.

Nature isn't the only place where you can find this pattern. The ancient Greeks thought the mathematical arrangement of the Fibonacci rectangle was one of the most beautiful forms in the world. They even called the Fibonacci rectangle the Golden Rectangle. The Greeks used this arrangement of small to large shapes in much of their architecture and artwork.

Mathematicians and scientists are still finding ways that Fibonacci numbers and nature overlap.

This nautilus shell has been cut in half to show the spaces inside.

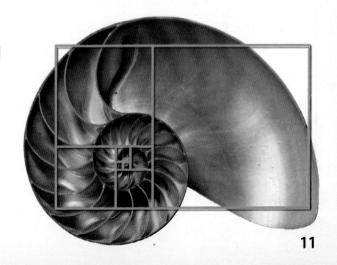

Responding

1. How are Fibonacci numbers formed?

2. What are the missing numbers in the pattern below?

0, 1, 1, 2, 3, _____, 8, 13, 21, 34, 55, _____,
144, 233, 377, _____, 987, . . .

3. Note Important Details What is one example of the Fibonacci series appearing in nature?

Activity

Nature is not the only place where Fibonacci numbers appear. Some writers use these numbers as a pattern for their writing.

Here is an example of a Fibonacci poem.
Line 1, 1 syllable: Math
Line 2, 1 syllable: ranks
Line 3, 2 syllables: as my
Line 4, 3 syllables: favorite
Line 5, 5 syllables: subject to study.
Line 6, 8 syllables: The rules make order from chaos.

Now you try. Write your own Fibonacci poem.